REFLECTION

REFLECTION

DERRICK MOORE

Dedication

I want to dedicate REFLECTION to my family and friends who have been my village. Your unwavering love has always been there to push me to be everything that God is calling me to be. To my parents, Deacon Fred and Missionary Mary Moore – thank you for teaching me about Christ at a young age. You all raised eleven children in the fear and admonition of the Lord, and I'm grateful to be one of them. To my church family, both former and present (Day's Temple COGIC, Forrest City, AR and Living Word COGIC, Waco, TX).

To the memory of the late Bishop John Henry Jennings and Mother Matlena Jennings. And also the late Evangelist Joyce Rodgers. I will never forget the many lessons I learned from each of you. May the ministry that the Lord has entrusted me with forever carry the fervor that I've seen in you.

Table of Contents

Forward

By: Dr. Gilbert Gillum Jr.

I am very proud of Derrick. I knew that he was an
exceptional young man when we first met. The one thing
that impressed me most was his humility of spirit. But I
wasn't only impressed by his humility. I was also
impressed by his musical skills on the Hammond organ
and keyboard. I also noticed that he carried himself
masterfully and recognized that he was a worshipper and
not just a musician.

His music created an atmosphere so that those who
listened could enter into a place where the spirit of God
flowed freely. It was a noticeable difference between him
and many others gifted to play music. We're living in a day
and time that so many musicians are very talented, but
there is a gap between their music and their dedication to
the God that they play and sing to. Derrick is a Man of
God first and then a musician. He is a prayer warrior and
a worshipper.

It stands to reason why this music and this book call
those who listen and read to grasp prayerfulness. It seems

to be latent throughout this document. It seems to me that the Holy Spirit is speaking through Derrick to bring us back to two essential things for the people of God in this season – prayer and worship. This book will be a guide for years to come.

I believe that this book is a must-read. It not only speaks to musicians or any other particular group. It transcends age, denomination, ethnicity. Instead, this book speaks to the entirety of the body of Christ. It is transformational. If you want to transform or bring transformation to your life of worship and prayer, this book is for you. The masses need it in their libraries. Not as just another book on the shelf, but one that will serve as a platform that catapults you into that next level in your relationship with Christ.

Introduction

When the Lord impressed upon me to write this book, it was given to accompany a handpicked set of songs that were given to encourage the saints. It was His will that I do not include songs that were geared directly toward Him (The Lord) in praise, but rather songs that spoke of Him, His ways, and His word that would encourage His people. This coincided with the Word of God that said to... "Let the word of Christ dwell in you richly in all wisdom; teaching and admonishing one another in psalms and hymns and spiritual songs, singing with grace in your hearts to the Lord." (Colossians 3:16 KJV)

While preparing to record this album, I desired to include songs of Praise on it that would be intimately sung before and to the LORD, but the Lord had another plan. He revealed to me that he had grown tired of EMPTY praises and that some had chosen to settle for the "sound of praise" and had forsaken having a "heart of praise." He also revealed to me that we, as a generation, have become more like those mentioned in Matthew 6:7, which "think they will be heard because of their many words." (Msg) Our worship to God is being filled with many different adjectives to describe Him as well as many different names (even in other languages) to call Him. But the real question is, "Do we really know Him." The King James Version called the people heathens who committed such acts in the verse mentioned. This word simply signifies that the person guilty of this does not know God.

There is a genuine problem when lives are lived more loosely, yet the lyrics we sing while we worship intensify. It is the epitome of what our Lord Jesus said when He stated... "This people draweth nigh unto me with their mouth, and honoureth me with their lips; But their heart is far from me." (Matthew 15:8 KJV) This is the true embodiment of what it means to be a hypocrite. When one draws closer to God with their hearts, they get to know Him. Not just know about Him, but they really know Him. This knowledge that is obtained by the spirit through prayer and the word of God that empowers our praise and our song. Trying to do it any other way makes one an imposter, a phony, and a counterfeit in the sight of God.

This is disheartening specifically because one has to remember that God is the one who matters most. If we are not seeking to please Him, our song, our praise, and our life won't amount to very much. The only way to please God is to give Him what He desires. And the only way to know what He wants is to seek Him in prayer and be consistent in reading His word. Many are using their own preconceived ideas of who God is and attempting to worship the "idol" that they've created rather than reading the word of God to find out who He really is and what He desires.

As we read the word and learn more about Him, his likes and dislikes, we realize that we can't stay where we are and please Him. We can't remain sinners (ones that practice sin). We have to be "transformed by the renewing of our minds." (Romans 12:2 KJV). After this transformation takes place, we then must "grow in grace and in the knowledge of our Lord and savior, Jesus Christ..." (2 Peter 3:18) It is through reading the word that we not only find out who we are and what belongs to us, but also what we must do to be to attain our belongings.

These belongings even include our final reward; heaven. To make it to heaven in the end and enjoy the blessings of God while on earth, one must do it according to the way that has been made plain through His Word, the Holy Bible. This word lets me know that if I want to please God, I must love Him and through this love be "conformed to the image of His Son." (Romans 8:28-29) I must become His Reflection.

This is the basis of this devotional book and the album that it coincides with. This book is for those who seek a true and pure relationship with God. It's specifically for those in transitional periods in their walk with God. For each song on the album, a chapter in the book parallels it. This will help give a more profound revelation and understanding of the lyrics to each song and provide an in-depth study, prayer, and meditation that allows one to connect and apply it to their own personal lives and be strengthened in whatever they are going through.

Prayer

"Lord, it's my prayer that each reader feels your presence while reading this book. I pray that while reading it that each one draws closer to you. Let them be strengthened with each line. Let it be Rhema in their hearts. Let them be encouraged to know that they are not walking by themselves but that You are with them. I thank You that You will keep them reminded of the indisputable fact that You CAN NOT fail and that they too can walk in victory in You. That though impossible in the flesh, in You, they can be conformed to Your image and become a true reflection of who You are. And we give You glory, honor, and praise. In Jesus' Name. Amen"

REFLECTION

CHAPTER ONE

Have Your Way (Prayer)

Have Your Way (Prayer)

Words and Music by: Derrick Moore
For Soul Reaching Publishing

Verse 1

Have Your way in me is my prayer

Have Your way in me is my prayer

Have Your way in me is my prayer

Have your way in me

Have Your way in me

Verse 2

I will say yes to Your will

I will say yes to Your will

I will say yes to Your will

Have Your way in me.

Have Your way in me.

Verse 3

I will say yes to Your way

I will say yes to Your way

I will say yes to Your way

Have Your way in me.

Have Your way in me.

"Father, we're coming to you, not asking you for houses, cars, and money. We're not even asking you for healing and deliverance. We're coming in pursuit of a deeper relationship with you. We've come seeking to look like our Father. We want to be His reflection.

Father, we know that there is no way to go through all that is necessary to look like You and reverberate Your reflection in the earth without first decreasing so that You may increase. (John 3:30) This transformation is too great for us to attempt on our own. We know that we must become detoxed and sober of ourselves, our thoughts, and even our desires. We must yield to You. You said in Your word that if any man comes after You, he must first deny himself. And Father, that's why we call on You now. (Luke 9:23)

We're in Your presence, asking You to have your way. In fact, I pray personally that You "have Your way in me." I open myself up to You and the process You designed for my transformation. I come limp in your presence, not simply as a sign of my weakness to your power but also as a sign of my trust in your plan. My heart desires to please You. My will desires for someone to see You through me. Lord, have your way!

We say yes to Your will and yes to Your way. It may not always feel so good and cause discomfort, but just as was said in the garden of Gethsemane, *"not my will, but thine, be done."* (Luke 22:42 KJV) When I'm challenged to resort back to the old me and my old actions, I'll say yes, Lord. I only ask that you do like you did Christ and send angels to strengthen me as I go through. You said in Your word that You hadn't forsaken them that seek you. (Psalm 9:10) And I'm so glad that You never change. You're yet dependable.

Now that we've established that you're dependable, we ask that you have your way to establish that dependability in us. We want You to depend on us not to give up in tough times. We also want You to depend on us to be Your reflection in the earth. Lord, give us to stay on the potter's wheel. As times get rough, give us to continue going through our tests, trials, and tribulations. So that the world can see You through us and come to know who You are for themselves. Rather than looking at the troubles of the world and even the troubles of those in the church, I ask that You do it in me. I surrender to You, Your will, and Your plan. Lord, make me Your reflection. This I pray in Jesus' name, Amen."

Reflection

CHAPTER TWO

Reflection

<u>Reflection</u>

Words and Music by: Derrick Moore
For Soul Reaching Publishing

<u>Chorus</u>

May my life be a reflection of who you are.

Be a reflection; of who you are.

<u>Verse</u>

Thinking on the other day about how good You are.

I messed up time after time, but you never left me in

the dark.

You've been so merciful and longsuffering.

That's why I present my body as a living offering.

I wanna walk like you.

I wanna talk like you.

<u>Bridge</u>

I'm not where I wanna be.

But thank God, I'm not where I use to be.

Everyday Lord; my desire is to be pleasing to thee.

I can't do it by myself.

But God I need Your help.

That's why I'm asking you to...

<u>Vamp</u>

Work on me (work on me) 4x Work on me. Work on

me

Say yes (yes) 4x Work on me. Work on me.

Particular objects give off a reflection. Some of the most common things that one might consider are mirrors, polished metal, glass, and water. The shiny nature of these objects allows them to have this reflective property. These objects, listed above, deal with what's technically known as specular reflection. This only happens when the object is so smooth that the light reflects at the same angle that it hits the surface. With light hitting at the same angle, it produces a reflection that is not distorted of whatever is in front of that object. When one goes to an object and looks in it for their reflection they are looking for just that, their reflection. If that object doesn't give off their reflection, it is proof, technically, that either the light is not hitting it or that it is an absorber of light.

This principle applies to the spiritual as well. If one is to be a reflection of Christ, the first necessary thing is that they must be made out of the appropriate material. This happens only when He (Christ) creates a new and clean heart in them. (Psalms 51) After that, to ensure that there is no distortion of His image, they must be placed on the potter's wheel, through reading the word and prayer, to be molded into who God would have for them to be—

making smooth every rough edge that would alter the image in any way. After all of this, one must have the right thing in front of them. Any suitable mirroring object will only produce the reflection of whatever is in front of it. If it produces something else, it's not considered a reflection. Technically, if light can't reflect off of it but absorbs all of the light instead, it will not be visible to the eye.

There was one in scripture who didn't want to reflect the image of God. His name was Lucifer. His name meant the "one that brings light" or the "morning star." The significance of the morning star is that it is one of the more giant planets, such as Venus, that shines bright early in the morning as the sun reflects upon it. Being the morning star, it served as a forerunner signifying that the greater light, the sun, was coming. This was Lucifer's job. Ezekiel 28:13-15 lets us know how God allowed Lucifer to be on the holy mountain. He even built instruments of tambourines and pipes inside of him so that he could go before Him. His job was to make known that the Great One was coming behind him. He continued in this position until he tried to make himself equal with the great light that he was supposed to be only introducing. The 15th verse lets us know that he was perfect from the day he

11

was created until iniquity was found in him. This iniquity was his demise. This was when Jesus said, "... I beheld Satan as lightning fall from heaven." Luke 10:18b KJV

To understand it more, one must even look at Lucifer's name in Hebrew. In Hebrew, his name was Halal or Helel. Halal, one form of his name meant to praise, boast, or celebrate. The other form of his name, Helel, meant a shining one or star. These both serve as the root word for the word "hallelujah." This word (hallelujah) actually has a dual meaning. In simple form, it means "praise (Hallel) ye the Lord (Jah)." But in its original Hebrew form, it's broken down to mean further "the star is God." This word makes plain and removes all confusion about who the glory belongs to. It all belongs to God.

Satan messed up when he stopped reflecting the light and became an absorber of the it. Ezekiel acknowledged that he got caught up in his own beauty. When he was consumed by these thoughts and tried to make himself equal to God, he was stripped of his name and kicked out of heaven. He was never known as Lucifer (the morning star) again, but rather as Satan (the adversary). According to scripture, he was kicked down to the ground and exposed before kings. The name Halal is no longer known to man without the other part of the word "-ujah," which lets us know that all praise belongs to God. With the believer being created by God, they must remain aware that they exist to give Him glory. All of it! They are not absorbers. That's the way of Satan (the adversary). But if they intend to remain in the favor of God, they must be reflectors. This is not a suggestion. This is an expectation for every believer and saint of God. It is not an expectation that is rooted and grounded in tradition alone, but this is the expectation of God.

"And Jesus answered them, saying, The hour is come, that the Son of man should be glorified. Verily, verily, I say unto you, Except a corn of wheat fall into the ground and die, it abideth alone: but if it die, it bringeth forth much fruit." (John 12:23-24 KJV)

In this passage of scripture, our Lord Jesus is speaking of the fact that He is about to be glorified through being lifted up on the cross. He told of the corn of wheat falling to the ground and dying. He was speaking of Himself and His purpose. This lets us know why He came to earth and what He had to fulfill. After stating His purpose, he states His why. He says that if the corn of wheat doesn't fall to the ground and die, it will exist alone.

But if it dies, it will bring forth much fruit. This not only tells us why He had to die, but this scripture also gives a unique insight into the expectations of Christ concerning every believer. Jesus said that if that seed dies (speaking of Himself), it would bring forth much fruit.

According to Genesis 1:11-12, everything God created brought forth fruit after its own kind. This meant that the fruit would have the same characteristics as the seed that it came from. For example, an apple seed can only yield apples, an orange seed, oranges, etc. Therefore since Christ became that seed that went into the ground, every fruit that He yields or produces can only be Christians with his characteristics. The only fruit that Christ can produce is Christ-like fruit. We have to reflect Him of whom we've come.

As saints and believers, one must not just strive to be any kind of reflector but a specular reflector. Remember, it was stated earlier that a specular reflection is when the light reflects at the same angle that it hits the surface. This keeps one from having a distorted view of the object being reflected. As believers, we must make sure that when Christ and even the world look at us, they are getting a clear image of who Christ is. This means that everything about us must reflect Him. We have to look like Him in our works, love, and even suffering.

The first way that we must look like Christ is in our works. The book of Genesis, even though speaking of the natural man, states that we were created in His image and His likeness. When we are converted and are saved, we take on His spiritual image and likeness. That means that we not only look like Christ, but we act like Him also. This means that we do the same things and works that He did. John 14:12 says, "Verily, verily, I say unto you, He that believeth on me, the works that I do shall he do also; and greater works than these shall he do; because I go unto my Father." This proves the scripture from earlier that lets us know that because he was the seed that went into the ground and is constantly producing more fruit, we would do greater works in quantity than He did. Romans 8:16-17 confirms this by letting us know that we are children of God. It further tells us that we are His heirs and joint-heirs with Christ. This means that whatever Christ has, we also have. This includes the power to heal the sick, cast out devils, and tread upon dangerous peril in His name without being harmed. If we are the fruit of Christ, it is imperative that we look like Him in works.

The second way that we must look like Christ is in our love. John 15:12 says, "This is my commandment, that you love one another as I have loved you." We have been admonished throughout scripture to love as Christ has loved us. Ephesians 5:2 even says, "And walk in love, as Christ loved us and gave himself up for us, a fragrant offering and sacrifice to God." We have to reflect Christ's love. The reality is that the love that we show to humankind can ofttimes be the greatest representation of Christ in the land. The most significant complication of our love is our forgiveness. We can't look like Christ in our love unless we learn to forgive like Him. This is arguably the tallest hurdle that our love will face. But if we are to reflect Christ in the way that we love, we have to learn to forgive. Ephesians 4:32 says... "and be ye kind one to another, tenderhearted, forgiving one another, even as God for Christ's sake hath forgiven you." Paul further wrote and said, "forbearing one another, and forgiving one another, if any man have a quarrel against any: even as Christ forgave you, so also do ye." (Colossians 3:13 KJV) Forgiveness is so important to God that Jesus told us that if we don't forgive others, our father will not forgive us (Matthew 6:14-15). It is impossible to fine-tune our reflection of Christ without making sure that we look like Him in our love.

The third way that we must reflect Christ is in our suffering. This is probably the least appealing part of the Christian walk from the onlooker's perspective and the immature. As we grow in God's grace, we realize that the suffering, though it doesn't feel good, really makes us and proves us. This is what makes it necessary. And because we are a reflection of Christ, and He suffered on the cross, we must go through our suffering as well. 1 Peter 4:1 says, "Forasmuch then as Christ hath suffered for us in the flesh, arm yourselves likewise with the same mind: for he that hath suffered in the flesh hath ceased from sin;" Paul took it a step further in Galatians 2:20. Here he says… "I have been crucified with Christ. It is no longer I who live, but Christ who lives in me. And the life I now live in the flesh I live by faith in the Son of God, who loved me and gave himself for me." As much as we wish and pray that it was possible, there is absolutely no way to be saved and omit suffering. 2 Timothy 3:12 says, "Yea, and all that will live godly in Christ Jesus shall suffer persecution." (KJV)

The amazing thing is that if we suffer like Christ, we can't just be found guilty of going through. Instead, how we go through matters just as much. 1 Peter 2 tells us that while Christ went through, he remained sinless; there was no guile found in his mouth, he didn't revile or threaten. This is so hard to fathom in today's society. While living in what one can consider the "clap back" society, it has become the norm to respond to, not to endure, and retaliate for any treatment that seems slightly harsh or slightly unfair. But here, our Lord and Savior suffered after having done no wrong without mistreating or responding negatively to anyone that wronged Him. We can't go with the standard of the day. We might feel gratified within ourselves if we do, but God will not be glorified. If we intend to reflect an image of Christ that is not distorted, we must learn to look like Him in our suffering.

The word reflection itself deals with giving back an image. If one only shows who they are and are wrapped up in themselves, they are not giving back the image of another. So if one is to be the reflection of Christ, they must give back His image instead of their own. The way they work, love, and suffer must look just like how Christ works, loves, and suffered. These three characteristics must be exemplified in the life of every believer. This is the only way that others can see Christ through them. They must become His reflection.

Are you able to do it on your own? Are you able to become a reflection of Him with just your own self-discipline and willpower? The truth is that you probably know the answer to this question better than I can tell you what it is. If you are like me, you've tried several times in your own strength. My reality is that I have to painstakingly admit that I've not had one successful attempt on my own. I've failed every time, beat myself up many times, and dealt with what seemed like a spiritual glass ceiling that I couldn't break due to these failed attempts.

It took a long time before I pinpointed the problem with my posture. The problem was that I was trying to do it all independently. I was trying to be His reflection in my own strength. To grow beyond the point where I was, I had to come to a realization that would alter the course of my life forever. The reality of it all is that I don't have the power to keep myself. He is the one that empowers me to work like Him, love like Him, and even suffer like Him. I had to realize that He, through the Holy Spirit (Holy Ghost), actually lived on the inside of me. In fact, I also had to realize that no one could reflect Him better than He could reflect Himself. I had to learn to surrender to His Spirit and allow Him to live through me. I had to realize that He is the only one that can present me faultless before the presence of His glory.

Prayer

"Dear Father. We thank you for the immutable fact that you are the Great Light. No one compares to You. They never can, neither will they ever be able to compare to you. You are God. Though we are not on your level and never will attempt to be, You still commanded us to be imitators of You in Your word. God, as we attempt to imitate You and be Your reflection, we acknowledge our humanity and that we need your help. We need You to empower us and strengthen us for this great task. We don't want to yield a distorted image of who You are. You're too good for that. You're too big for that. And You deserve better than that. We desire to give You what you desire. We want to reflect your glory in every way. We want You to be seen in our works, in our love, and our suffering. Help us, Lord. We present our bodies as a living sacrifice to You. We realize that we can't do it on our own. Therefore, we surrender to You. We come to You saying yes to Your will. Yes, to Your way. Yes, Lord. We welcome Your Holy Spirit to take over. So that You can continue to work in us, both to will and to do according to Your own good pleasure. Help us in this transformation. We've started with You, and we intend to go all the way. In Jesus' name, we pray. Amen."

Reflection

CHAPTER THREE

Every Word You Say

Every Word You Say
Words and Music: Derrick Moore
For Soul Reaching Productions

Verse 1

So heavy laden, feels like I'm fading

and the room is spinning. But I won't lose my balance

Cause I still have a word

Verse 2

That Word is from You. Tested, tried, and true.

No matter what You always come through.

That's why I won't lose my balance,

Because I still have a word.

Chorus

When I can't see my way

Don't know how I'll make it through another day

I'll trust You Lord (and I'll believe) Every Word You

say

2x and Modulate

Vamp
Every Word You say

Repeat Chorus 2x

"But he answered and said, It is written, Man shall not live by bread alone, but by every word that proceedeth out of the mouth of God."

(Matthew 4:4 KJV)

Words! Words! Words! One's words are one of the most underrated tools in the toolbox that man uses. There are two forms of communication. They are verbal and nonverbal. Both are defined by whether or not they use words. Nonverbal communication is done without words, while verbal requires the use of sounds and words to exist. People don't realize that their words carry as much power as they do. The bible declares, "Death and life are in the power of the tongue:" (Proverbs 18:21a KJV). God gave man this much power in His words.

But if man possesses this much power in his words, imagine the power that God has in His. God spoke in the book of Genesis and created light, seas, dry land, plants, the sun, moon, birds, and beasts with His words. All this happened simply because He uttered the words "let there be." His words are the ultimate authority of all that exists.

If He calls it to be, there is an absolute zero percent chance of it not happening. If God said it, it's inevitable.

Knowing that His Word is ultimate, and He is omniscient and full of wisdom, He chooses all of His words wisely. God has never been wasteful. He doesn't waste any time, experiences, or words. He has a purpose with everything. What looks to be wasted time and everything else that we go through has been planned by God. He has carefully plotted it out and determined that it all will work together for your good if you "love Him and are called according to His purpose." (Romans 8:28 KJV)

Throughout scripture, the Lord used His voice to speak to man. He would use it to give and communicate instructions, speak promises based on covenant, affirm, encourage, bring change, and many other things. If one has learned anything from the creation story in the book of Genesis, it's that the voice of the Lord demands a response. Like everything else that God created, man has to respond to His Word. Man has to remain cognizant that great responsibility comes with the privilege of having the Word of God. Though God gave him the ability to operate according to his own free will, He yet demands him to listen, respond, and obey the words that He speaks.

"What are you doing with what God has spoken to you?"

Have you ever given anyone instructions only to realize that they didn't hear all of it and began functioning according to a fraction of what was stated or completely manipulated what was said to mean something altogether different? How did that make you feel? Were you frustrated? Did they follow the instructions that you gave? The answers to these questions respectively should be yes, bad, yes, and no.

These responses cause me to raise the question of how God feels when we do the same thing. Though He gives precise instructions in His Word, we often either only listen to part of it or even have the audacity to manipulate what He says to mean something altogether different. Some even choose to ignore His instructions to do their own thing entirely. He must feel very frustrated and angry for His Word to be taken lightly. In fact, He said in His Word, "What thing soever I command you, observe to do it: thou shalt not add thereto, nor diminish from it." (Deuteronomy 12:32 KJV) He instructs in this verse first to observe it. Observing it means paying close attention to it and persistently doing it. Then he admonishes them not to alter what he said. Anytime God gives specific instructions, it is to yield a particular result. When one adds to it or subtracts from what He stated, they can't expect to receive the outcome that He has reserved for those who obey Him.

This is a season where many try to make up their own set of principles to be governed by and expect God to honor them. They operate without having a mental or moral center to keep them grounded. Conspiracy theories are at an all-time high. Mental instability is so prevalent. This instability is seen in the number of people taking medicine for mental imbalance and the suicide rate. So many don't know what to think. And in the midst of all of this confusion, social media (though a great source for connecting and ministry) has given everyone a platform and a voice. While it rightfully levels the playing field by giving everyone a chance to be heard, it brings with it the opportunity to manipulate the minds of those that are not grounded in the Word of God. The confused are confusing others.

Many individuals become susceptible to many of these unfounded arguments simply because they can be either argued well, quantified in a way that the mind can understand and validate, or merely because they're looking for something new. This is not anything unexpected and alarming for the believer to see. Paul prophesied this in his 2nd Epistle to Timothy when he said, "For the time will come when they will not endure sound doctrine; but after their own lusts shall they heap to themselves teachers, having itching ears; and they shall turn away their ears from the truth, and shall be turned unto fables." (2 Timothy 4:3-4 KJV)

How we respond to the instructions of God matters. It determines our identity. God meant for us to be established in Him and not merely exist. He desires us to be like a tree. This is proven in the first Psalm that David penned. He writes.:

"Blessed is the man that walketh not in the counsel of the ungodly, nor standeth in the way of sinners, Nor sitteth in the seat of the scornful. But his delight is in the law of the LORD; And in his law doth he meditate day and night. And he shall be like a tree planted by the rivers of water,

That bringeth forth his fruit in his season; His leaf also shall not wither; And whatsoever he doeth shall prosper." Psalm 1:1-3 KJV

In this passage, David compares us to being like a tree. This is a loaded analogy. Referring to one as a tree symbolizes them possessing strength, stability, growth, and prosperity. For David to compare the man mentioned in Psalm 1 to a tree, he says that the man will walk in those same characteristics. He will have strength, stability, growth, and prosperity.

Also, in the passage, David speaks of the tree being planted by rivers of water. The water represents The Word of God in the analogy. It symbolizes life that is given to all that touch it. The water makes the land rich in minerals that provide nutrients that serve as food that enhances growth for anything planted in it.

To further understand what David was saying, one must realize that there is a relationship between the water and the tree. The water is the source that gives life to the tree. It even provides the minerals in the soil around the tree used to make its food. The reality is that the water could exist without the tree, but the tree can't live without

31

the water. The tree will soon dry up, wither up, and die without the water. Just as it is with the water and the tree, this is how our relationship works with the Word. The Word is the way by which we grow. It is the life-giving source. Unlike the Word, which can exist without us, we cannot exist without the Word. Without the Word, we, like the tree, can't survive. We will ultimately dry up, wither up, and die.

For this relationship between the water and the tree to function appropriately, something must connect the two. This connector would be the root system. It is the roots that grow first and over time continue to expand. They allow the tree to absorb the water and transport it to the rest of the tree so that it may grow and sustain life. If one notices how roots look on a tree, they will see how they appear as if they are actually reaching. They are extending from the tree, searching for something to sustain life.

This is true even in David's analogy in Psalm 1. The roots represent man's delight and meditation. Just as the roots connect the tree to the water, meditation connects the man to the Word. For the man to grow, he has to have a way to absorb the Word and transport it into every part of his life. This takes place through his meditation on it. David said that this man who meditated day and night would be like that tree whose leaves would not wither and who would be productive. With its leaves not withering, it proved that it had Word to be sustained consistently and continually. The tree's productivity speaks of its ability to produce fruit. And since a tree cannot consume its fruit, it's only logical to conclude that David is saying that just as trees, we will have enough supply to be a blessing to someone else. It is only through the root system that a tree can take in enough water to produce these kinds of results.

With this knowledge, one can properly assess that many trees are struggling to survive because they have dysfunctional relationships with the water. Some are dysfunctional in that they are too far from the water. These are those whose minds are wandering far from the Word of God. Some minds are meditating on their problems rather than meditating on the Word. Other minds are meditating on possessions, distractions, and other idols they have erected. Regardless of what one may focus on, they become malnourished without meditating and receiving the water that the river of the Word provides.

And if one goes too long without connecting with the river, they will die.

Another dysfunctional relationship that many have with the water is that they don't want to go through a process called pruning. You might wonder what the pruning process has to do with the water. Pruning of a tree takes place when one cuts away the parts of the tree that will not receive the water. These are the parts of the tree that are dead. If trees fail to be pruned, it proves that someone either got lazy or liked the tree in its current state without wanting it to continue growing. Either way, pruning is yet necessary. This deadwood, produced from the lack of water flow, becomes weight that the tree carries. "Wherefore seeing we also are compassed about with so great a cloud of witnesses, let us lay aside every weight, and the sin which doth so easily beset us, and let us run with patience the race that is set before us," (Hebrews 12:1 KJV) This is why pruning is necessary. Whether in a race or on a tree, weight serves as a hindrance that must be laid aside for one to proceed in an uninhibited manner. If this weight is not removed, deadness caused by the lack of water or even disease can spread to the rest of the tree and cause the entire tree to die.

If one pays close attention, they will realize that each of these dysfunctions have an end result of death. The critical point to bring out is that we can't survive without meditating on the Word of God. This fixed position of meditation allows us to walk consistently in life. This life doesn't cease to exist because of the winds that blow so vehemently. Neither does it end because of the storms that may come. Trees planted by the rivers of water can stand the test of time. They are strong.

This is how we must be with our meditation of the Word of God. That is the only way that we'll be able to recall the Word during the times when the storms of life are raging. Sometimes walking with the Lord may seem so hard and sometimes not worth it because of the storms that we're in. But when we meditate on the Law (His Word) both day and night, we're able to walk into a strength that others have yet to know. This is possible because we can recall scripture that applies to our situations during our time of need. We can recall the words of David when he said, "Bless the LORD, O my soul, And forget not all His benefits:" (Psalm 103:2 KJV).

In the 69th number of the same book, He also declared that God loads us daily with benefits.

But while remembering the promises of God, we must be careful. The problem with many in this current day and time is that they read the Word to highlight the promises that God made to man instead of developing a relationship with the one who made the promises. This is done through prayer and reading His Word. For some, this is an issue. They don't consider His instructions or commandments. They don't realize that God has always been more concerned about their relationship and development with Him than He was concerned about the perks and benefits of the relationship. Maybe this is why many of today's worship songs speak of God's commitment to us rather than our commitment to Him. When we become committed and develop an appropriate relationship with Him through His Word, we will become more relationship-driven and not give up so easily when strong winds begin to blow in our lives.

As we develop proper relationships with God through His Word, we will begin to apply it to every situation in our lives. This will be inevitable because it will become what we meditate on day and night. This is what will cause us to faith it rather than fear it. This is what will cause us to walk by faith and not by sight. The situation won't matter as much because we will realize that the Word will trump it all. This Word will keep us grounded and centered. It will keep us from panicking and becoming anxious. It will give us a settling and a peace amid the storm. When we become consistent with meditating day and night, we won't cherry-pick the Word for the parts that we like best and for what seems advantageous to our feelings. Instead, we will trust, believe, and rely on "every word You say."

Prayer

"Father, we first come to You repenting of how we've focused on everything else without giving You and Your Word the attention that is deserved. But God, we thank You for the opportunity and grace to get back on the right path. Thank You for Your revelation that makes us aware of who we are and the relationship we are supposed to have with You. I ask now that You build us up where we've been torn down and give us to focus on You like never before. I thank You that You are God, and You are the same. You don't change. You're dependable. And we can rely on Your dependability and the dependability of Your Word. Give us to keep our testimony through the storm, rain, heartaches, and pain. Let that testimony be that... Even "when I can't see my way, and don't know how I'll make it through another day. I'll trust You; Lord, and I believe every word You say." In Jesus' name, we pray.

Amen"

CHAPTER FOUR

Satisfy

Satisfy

Words and Music by: Derrick Moore
For Soul Reaching Publishing

Verse 1

So many people are so depressed today.

Wondering will God do it; Will he make a way.

He wants to do it today, but you're just too far away.

(Come closer to Him and be satisfied)

Verse 2

Abhor that which is evil and cleave to that which is good.

My God will make a way just like he said He would.

Separate yourself from sin, and don't forget to come closer

to Him.

(Come closer to Him and be satisfied)

Chorus

(He will do it.) He will deliver your soul.

(He will do it.) From that thing that won't let you go.

(He will do it.) He'll bring peace to your troubled mind.

(He will do it.) He'll come through just in the nick of time.

(He won't leave you where you are) Just come close to

God

Repeat Chorus

<u>Vamp</u>

Satisfy (8x)

Come (7x)

My understand that to be like Christ, they must give up all that is not like Him. They have to let go of every sinful deed and desire. The reality is that everyone feels differently about the sins that they had to relinquish for the sake of Christ. This feeling is often contingent upon how the individual felt about sin at the moment of conversion. To some, their sins may have been fun and fulfilling. While to others, their sins brought a sense of fatigue and weariness. These feelings cames about by how the individual had grown tired of them and the trouble they've brought. They gladly gave them up in hopes of finding a better way. In both circumstances, both types of individuals give up their sin to follow this better way, which is Christ.

Ironically, there's an issue that seems to be plaguing so many that have given up sin to follow Christ. Many seem to have a void in their lives even though they've accepted Christ. This void exists because of removing what that individual once looked to for fulfillment. They are not satisfied. That individual is dealing with what seems to be lack. They carry salvation as a burden rather than the privilege that it is. They view serving God as an obligation rather than something that they should do willingly and joyfully.

Why is this so? How is it even possible? How can it be possible to give up everything in this world to serve God, only to be left feeling miserable? How can it be possible after Jesus stated, "...Verily I say unto you, There is no man that hath left house, or brethren, or sisters, or father, or mother, or wife, or children, or lands, for my sake, and the gospel's, but he shall receive an hundredfold now in this time, houses, and brethren, and sisters, and mothers, and children, and lands, with persecutions; and in the world to come eternal life." (Mark 10:29-30 KJV) So why is it that so many feel empty, unrewarded, and unsatisfied?

Ironically, when Jesus said this, it was responding to Peter telling Him how they (the disciples) had given up everything to follow Him. His response was letting Peter know that it was obviously more for Him than what he was receiving. He told Peter that what He had for him was a hundred times greater than what he gave up. Knowing that the word of God is accurate, how can it be possible to be so unsatisfied after having given up so much to follow God? The answer to this question is much more straightforward than many believe and can be summed up into one word. That word is distance.

"... In thy presence is fulness of joy; At thy right hand there are pleasures for evermore." (Psalm 16:11 KJV) The satisfaction that many are looking for is only provided in His presence. This explains why so many are miserable even though they've given up so much. They aren't in His presence. That is where the fulness of joy is, and if one gets close enough, they can even get the pleasures that are in His right hand. Jesus even said in John 6:35 that whoever comes to Him will not hunger. This hunger represents that emptiness and dissatisfaction.

While writing this chapter, I was reminded of years ago. I would often go into prayer, expressing my grievances to God. I would speak my issues to him just like a man in a marriage who wasn't satisfied with the relationship he had with his wife. The reality was that I didn't view it as a relationship at the time of my expression. All I saw was what I wanted and what I felt like I lacked. This sentiment was what I expressed to God. I told Him about what I saw everyone else enjoying in life. I told Him about all the things that I gave up to be with Him. Then I told Him (in so many words) that I couldn't keep going like this.

I didn't realize how selfish I was until just now, as I am writing this. It never crossed my mind that I had made it entirely about myself. As if I were the one that mattered most. As if I were the only one that mattered. I didn't consider asking the Lord what He wanted and desired from me. Like any relationship, there is a need for requitement and reciprocation. In laymen's terms, this is to say that one has to give to get. Even though I felt like I had given up so much already to be with God, I had to realize that that was just for the sake of getting in the relationship. That part must be automatic to maintain my marriage with Him. I must remain unquestionably faithful to Him, forsaking all that would hinder our relationship.

But the question remains, now that we have married Christ, "how do we become satisfied and inspired enough to remain in the relationship?" I submit to you that the answer is in how the Lord answered me. When I would come to Him with my grievances of all I gave up to be with Him, He could have told me what all He gave up to be with me. I mean, He did endure the cross, all of the sufferings, the beatings, and even death just to be with me.

He could have even brought up all the times that I was unfaithful and cheated on Him. How I metaphorically slept around with the enemy and came back to Him expecting Him to act like nothing ever happened. And amazingly, that's precisely what He did every time.

Instead of throwing any of this in my face and responding harshly of any kind, the Lord responded the same way to me every time I would express my dissatisfaction. He would simply utter the words, "Come closer. Come closer to Me." Often I would get frustrated with God and further express my grievances to Him. He would only respond with the same words. "Come closer." I would even go to noonday prayer at Living Word Church of God in Christ (Waco, Tx) and try to do it where no one could hear me but Him. He would then speak directly through Mother Wilma Watts (the leader of this song), who would cry out loudly, "Come! Come! Closer! Closer to me!" With this not being the answer I wanted, I would often complicate the answer that He gave. I would often ask God, "how do I come closer?" This question would be accompanied by a whole series of other questions that I don't remember the Lord ever responding to.

He was so patient with me. He kept saying the same thing to me until, through my desperation, I came closer. With my distress, I had no other choice. I had reached a "sink or swim" moment in my walk with Christ. This moment was the catalyst that pushed me closer in prayer. Ironically, I began to notice that the closer I drew to Him, the closer He drew back to me. (James 4:8) Though it may seem cliché, I found out that His presence is sweet. I began to enjoy being close to Him. This closeness allowed me to feel His presence like I'd never experienced it before. This closeness alone satisfied me to the point that I no longer longed for what I gave up to be with God. His presence was enough to get me off of the edge of wanting to give up my relationship with Him. That no longer seems like an option. I would rather have Him than anything in this world.

Being close to Him not only satisfied me in that way, but it also became very satisfying for the Lord to reveal to me some of His secrets. Sometimes he would give insight on plans, needs of others, and even things that would happen the next day. It would be these things that would just blow my mind. It was me drawing closer that allowed me to really know Him and not just know of Him. The closer I drew, the more I realized that there is no limit to His power. The closer I drew, the more I realized how much He loves me. The closer I drew, the more I realized that my perspective was very obscure before drawing closer. Even though I am yet learning and coming closer, I must admit that what I've learned and received from God so far is enough to change my life forever.

It's from this corridor that I offer praise to Him continually. I, like David, feel compelled to command myself to bless the Lord at all times and let His praises repeatedly flow out of my mouth. I continually feel compelled to tell someone about His goodness and how great He is. But not only do I talk about Him, but I also talk to Him. I often tell Him how there is no one like Him anywhere. I love telling Him how much I love Him and how no one can come close to comparing to Him. I found out that drawing closer to Him increases even my praise to and about Him. The very thought of Him makes me say wonderful things about Him.

You may ask, "Why do I praise God the way that I do?" The answer is simply because I'm satisfied. Rather than complaining and expressing grievances, I began learning to love and appreciate Him when I started getting closer.

How do you feel about God and your walk with Him? Do you feel empty at times and lack satisfaction? Do you often reflect thinking that life would be so much better if you were still doing what you used to do, with who you did it with, before Christ? Do you struggle with holding on because of the emptiness and lack of satisfaction you sometimes feel? If you answered any of these questions by saying yes, I must tell you that you are too far from God. You really can give up things, people, and deeds for God and feel dissatisfied.

You have to "Come closer." You have to come close enough to hear His voice. Come close enough to feel His touch. Come close enough to see His face. Everything you need is in His presence. The lyrics to the song say: "He wants to do it today, but you're just too far away. Come closer to Him and be satisfied." No matter how great the dissatisfaction feels. Come closer, and you will see how small that feeling actually is. Remember that the way you feel represents only one-hundredth of what God wants to do for you. That's right—one hundredth. Come closer and find out what He has in store for you.

Prayer

"Father, in the name of Jesus: So many have been told what they have to give up, but many have been deprived of the knowledge that the gain is so much greater than the giving. Lord touch now. Change the mindset of those that are without understanding. Help them know that no one and nothing can ever satisfy as You can. Look upon that one that feels like giving up. Do for them as You said You would do in Your word. Satisfy the longing soul. (Psalm 107:9) Give them to draw closer so that they can hear You. Close enough that they can see You and feel You. They've experienced being far. That left them feeling so empty and even frustrated. So, God, they're coming to You because they want to be closer. While they are in Your presence, touch them, speak to them, and reveal to them. And they'll never be the same. With this encounter, they'll be inspired to do greater exploits for You and to tell the world about how great You are. This we ask in Jesus' name. Amen."

Reflection

CHAPTER FIVE

Stayed on You

<u>Stayed on You</u>
Words and Music by: Derrick Moore
For Soul Reaching Publishing

<u>Chorus</u>
My mind is stayed on You. My eyes are fixed on You.

When I've had enough, I'll just look up.

For my mind is stayed on You.

<u>Verse</u>
The distractions almost swept me away.

The tempter came and tried to shake my faith.

But Your peace is all I need. And I'll have it if I keep my

mind on Thee.

Modulate and Repeat Chorus

<u>Vamp</u>
Look up! I'll just look up.

I am standing on Your word. I believe what it says.

I'll just look up.

That's why I praise You. That's why I praise You.

That's why I praise You. I'm looking up.

I'm looking up. 4x

For my mind is stayed on You.

"O our God, wilt thou not judge them? for we have no might against this great company that cometh against us; neither know we what to do: but our eyes are upon thee."

2 Chronicles 20:12 KJV

T he word "stay" means to continue to be as specified. (dictionary.com) So to say that "my mind is stayed on You" (Christ) is to say that my mind continues to be on You. For some, it's easy to "put" one's mind on Christ in a time of need. They do it because they are in trouble and look to Him to pull them out. For others, it's easy to "put" one's mind on Christ when things are going the way they desire. They do it because of the gratitude in their hearts, realizing that no one but God has blessed them and allowed them to experience the high point that they're experiencing. What's problematic about this is that "putting" their mind on Christ only speaks of an instance and can change at any given moment.

As people of God, one must remember that the key is in the continuance. Paul even said that He is "a rewarder of them that diligently seek Him." (Hebrews 11:6) Here he speaks of those that continue and are persistent in their seeking. One's focus can't be based on their senses or circumstances. These two variables tend to work very well with another variable called time to cause one to become weary in well-doing and begin to doubt. Time is the variable that makes one tired of waiting for the manifestations of God. In contrast, the other two variables tend to parenthetically dangle either the promise or the unlikely fruition of it in one's face.

An example of this is in Matthew 14:25-31, when Peter walked on water. As long as he remained focused on Christ, everything was okay. Peter "put" his mind on Jesus and the word He had spoken to him when He told him to come and walk on the water. The problem came when Peter, through his sense of sight, saw the effects of the boisterous winds. When he did this, he became afraid and began to sink (Matthew 14:30)

Ironically, what Peter saw was enough to take his mind off what Christ said. The wind served as the variable of doubt that told him that he either couldn't or at least wasn't supposed to be walking on the water. This irony further confuses because Peter was already doing what the wind reminded him that he shouldn't be able to do.

God allowed Peter to do what no one else in scripture could do because he "put" His mind on Him. But at the same time, Peter began to drown because he didn't "keep" his mind on Him. Had Peter's mind been "stayed" or kept on Him, there's no telling the hurdles he would've overcome or the miraculous things he would've been able to accomplish. This story is proof that when trying to focus and keep your mind stayed on Christ, one must watch their senses. What one sees, hears, smells, and feels can take their attention and cause them to be distracted from what God has said and wants to manifest on their behalf.

The other variable that pairs well with time to bring doubt in the believer's mind is the circumstance. A biblical example of this is Zacharias, the husband of Elizabeth. (Luke 1:6-18) When the angel, Gabriel, came with the message of God that his wife was going to bear a son, he focused on his circumstance rather than what God said. He began to doubt because his wife was barren. And on top of her being barren, time became a factor. Not only was she barren, but both of them had gotten old.

Though it was true that Elizabeth was barren and they were both old, the actual problem was that he let their reality carry more weight than the word of God. Zacharias abandoned the infallibility of the word that was spoken and chose instead to embrace his circumstance. He lost focus because of his reality.

Like Peter and Zacharias, we can easily be dissuaded from focusing on God by our senses and circumstances. It's easy to "put" one's mind on God, but the key to keeping it on Him is contingent upon one's actions in the presence of disagreeing senses and circumstances. If one over listens, overthinks, overanalyzes, or even over gazes with their senses into their circumstances, they will end up walking in doubt and ultimately abandoning their focus on God.

Putting one's mind on God is easy, especially when they've heard of Him. But keeping one's mind on Him requires a tunnel vision that must manage coexisting with the noise of opposition. In fact, it's in these moments that one has to give extra effort to keep their mind "stayed on Him."

In the scripture mentioned at the beginning of this chapter, King Jehoshaphat and Judah are surrounded by their enemies who had joined forces into a super army against them. The interesting thing about this passage is that the author gives insight on not just what was going on but also how the King felt when he prayed while being surrounded. He brings to the Lord's attention in 2 Chronicles 20:10-11 that these were the same armies that He (the Lord) didn't permit them to invade and destroy and that now they had come to kick Judah out of their territory that had been promised to them. This was his assessment of the circumstance he had witnessed with his senses. After making this assessment, he then assesses his ability against his enemy. He acknowledges in verse 12 that they "have no might against this great company." He then further admits that they don't know what to do and then says, "but our eyes are upon thee." (2 Chronicles 20:12 KJV)

In the context of King Jehoshaphat's prayer, he admitted his inability but acknowledged that his eyes (which represented his focus) were fixed on God. It was when King Jehoshaphat and Judah acknowledged that their eyes were upon the Lord that He sent a word to tell them that the battle was not theirs but His and that they had no need to even fight in it. This very word that the Lord sent calmed their fears and moved God to fight on their behalf.

We often "put" our minds on God for a moment until the noise of our circumstances and senses start to enter the mix. Sometimes we seem surrounded. And not just by anyone. Like Jehoshaphat, we often feel surrounded by our enemies that the Lord has not yet graced us to invade and destroy. These tend to be the enemies that we have not yet conquered in life that sometimes seem to join forces and come at us simultaneously.

What do you do when it seems like all of your enemies have joined forces to attack you at the same time? What do you do when you feel overwhelmed by your situation and by what you sense about your current circumstance? Do you succumb to your reality or follow the example of King Jehoshaphat? Do you panic, or do you pray? Do you try to play the role of the fixer, or do you fix your focus on God and what He said?

Sometimes during the process of transformation into the new man that reflects the image of Christ, it becomes easy to resort back to what one knows before being converted. This is an acknowledgment that it requires extra effort to walk in the ways of the new man purposely. This is necessary until it becomes automatic and more habitual. Once the habit develops, it will become second nature and take over even when your mind wants to go contrary to it.

One example of this is when I attended college at Arkansas State University. My major was vocal music education. When I informed my vocal professor that I had issues with nervousness, her remedy was to increase my practice time. While I viewed this extra practice as punishment, she was privy to a knowledge that I had yet to learn. When I questioned her methods, she told me that with more practice, I would be able to do it right so much that my nervousness couldn't make me do it wrong.

This applies to our spiritual habits as well. If one gets used to focusing on God, their circumstances and senses wouldn't be able to take our minds off of Him. If one gets used to speaking blessings over those who mistreat them, no one would be able to make them use profanity concerning that individual. The same is true for those who create habits of praying when times get rough. They will learn to pray and talk to God rather than folding under pressure.

This is actually how Jesus ended up praying the infamous prayer in the garden of Gethsemane. In Luke 22, as Jesus is preparing to go to Calvary, He has a moment where His flesh is warring against His spirit. He tells His disciples to go and sell their goods and purchases swords with their sales profits. He even tells them why. Jesus says to them that "this that is written must yet be accomplished in me, and he was reckoned among the trangressor: for the things concerning me have an end" (Luke 22:37 KJV). Our Lord Jesus knew that His time was coming to an end but, through flesh, wanted to fight back because he realized the task was so great for Him. After the disciples only came back with two, he told them that that was enough.

That's when verse 39 picks up and says, "And He came out and went, as was His habit, to the Mount of Olives; and the disciples followed Him." (Luke 22:39 AMP) On top of this Mount, He went to the garden of Gethsemane where He prayed the prayer asking the Father to let this cup pass from Him. But then He ultimately says, "nevertheless not my will, but thine, be done." (Luke 22:42 KJV) After praying this prayer, an angel came from heaven and strengthened Him for the task at hand.

Many never mention these verses, but perhaps these are some of the most pivotal verses in all of scripture. Had Jesus not had a habit of prayer, He would have fought back and might not have made it to calvary. And if He had walked in His flesh and fought back, He might not have been blameless. Had He not made it to calvary, there would've been no resurrection. Without a resurrection, no one would be able to be saved. So perhaps, had it not been for His habit of prayer that led Him to Gethsemane, there would be no complete Gospel.

As saints of God, we must develop habits of keeping our minds stayed on Him. I'm reminded of the words of my former church mother, Mother Ella Beck, as she was bedridden but praying for another one of the saints and me. She said, "Lord give them the strength to take it to You every time." It's our ability to keep our mind stayed on Him that allows us to be a reliable reflection of Him. No one wants to look in a mirror that only reflects appropriately sometimes. This consistency and diligence will not only allow us to reliably reflect the image of Christ but will also allow us to see more of His desires and will for man to be manifested in the earth.

Prayer

"Father, in the name of Jesus, we come to You admitting that this is an area of struggle to many of us. We desire to be your reflection, but we know we can't reflect that which is out of our focus. We need your help. Help us and give us the strength to take it to You every time. Give us focus in the middle of the noise. Don't let us be swept away by distractions. Don't let the temptations shake our faith. Help us not just talk about You but also develop habits to build up our relationship with You. You're more than worthy of our love. More than worthy of our attention and affection. More than worthy of our trust. Strengthen us as we strive to trust You in everything and not lean on our own understanding. This we ask in Jesus' name. Amen."

Reflection

CHAPTER SIX

Call Jesus

Call Jesus
Words and Music: Derrick Moore
For Soul Reaching Productions

Verse

Who can you call when you need a friend? (I call on Him)

Who is the one on whom you can depend? (I call on Him)

Who can you call when you're going through? (I call on Him)

Who is the one who is able to carry you through?

I stand and proclaim that all you have to do is call His name.

Chorus

Oh oh oh, Oh oh oh

It's Jesus; It's Jesus

Oh oh oh, Oh oh oh

It's Jesus; It's Jesus

Repeat Verse

Repeat Chorus

Bridge

Call Him 8x

Vamp

Jesus 3x

Oh oh oh oh

Jesus

A call is defined as a cry made as a summons or to attract someone's attention. (dictionary.com) Generally speaking, there are several different reasons why one might call on the name of another.

Call Him in Our Feelings...

Some may call the name because they simply love how their name sounds. They can think of how that individual makes them feel affirmed, loved, or well taken care of, and it can heavily influence their desire to say that person's name often. However, others might call the name because that individual angers or frustrates them. These calls are made based on how the individual can make them feel.

When dealing specifically with the name of Jesus, those that have a relationship with him tend to sometimes call His name out of their affection. It is challenging to think on His goodness, His unconditional love, and His provision and not feel moved with affection for Him. When one calls on His name from this mental place, the relationship fuels the desire to call His name. When one feels so passionate and affectionate about the Lord Jesus, they don't even have to call His name loudly. There tends to be satisfaction with just a barely audible utterance of

His name. This is the call that is based on our feelings about Him.

Call Him in Conversation...

Some individuals may call the name of another for a completely different reason. They might do it because they want to get their attention to converse with them. In this situation, one calls the name for two reasons. One reason is that the individual with whom they are conversing is not confused about who is being talked to. The other reason that one calls the name during conversation is to focus directly on them as they speak to them. This allows the conversation to be sincere and brings about a more substantial level of intimacy that may not have otherwise existed.

This is the call that we make during our conversations with the Lord. The name that we give these conversations is called prayer. While we pray, we often call on the name of the Lord conversationally. It's very traditional in many denominations that are Christian-based to begin the prayer with, "Father, in the name of Jesus...." This is how we do what was previously expressed. Calling His name at the beginning of the prayer ensures there is no

71

confusion about who is being talked to in the conversation. Even though God is omniscient and is aware that He is being addressed, it's always appropriate to call someone's name and greet them when you start a conversation.

The other reason for calling Jesus' name during the conversation of prayer is when it is done in a moment where one feels like they need His full attention and focus. It's not as if the individual is not already talking to God, but this moment serves as a refresher to the conversation. It causes the one talking to feel that they have God's undivided attention. (Even though we know that God doesn't need it. It's more for the sake of the individual praying) They call His name to reassure that He hears what they are about to say in these moments. It removes noise and distractions from the conversation of prayer and allows one to feel that they have a direct line of contact with God.

Side note: I admonish every reader not to get so entangled in the legalisms and technicalities of prayer that they overlook its purpose to focus on that which matters least. God is more concerned that one continues in reverent, earnest, and diligent prayer. He cares about this more than one following a guidebook on praying and offering Him something that's not sincere.

Call Him when we need help...

Another time that one calls the name is when they cry for help. When one calls the name while they are in this situation, it is generally because they feel that the individual whose name they are calling is in a predicament where they can assist. When an individual calls the name as a cry for help, their motive can usually notice it in their voice's inflections. This inflection elevates either because of the panic that results from the situation they are trying to get out of or to alert the individual whose name they are calling to let them know that they are in dire need of their help. The voice will portray the desperation of the individual that is crying out.

The new testament is replete with examples of how individuals cried to the Lord for help. From the blind man who sat by the way begging (Luke 10:35-38) to Peter drowning after walking on water. (Matthew 14:28-30) There are plenty of examples of people who called on the Lord for help. I love that it not only showed people crying but also showed how God responded. It showed that He saved all that called on His name. It's consoling to know that God is faithful and does not fail.

When one calls the name of Jesus as a cry for help, they call Him because they believe that He can assist them in their predicament. They call Him because they know that He is "able help." He is the God that can actually do the impossible. His track record speaks for itself. While walking the earth, He raised the dead; He healed the sick, cast out devils, and even forgave sin. If He could do all of this and exercise His willingness to do all of that, one can rest in confidence that He is more than capable of handling whatever they are going through.

When individuals call on the Lord as a cry for help, they demonstrate their trust in Him. This is befitting, considering the ability that He has. He is the one that specializes in doing the impossible. Nothing is too hard for Him. It is also befitting assessing our posture as children of God. When a child gets in trouble or to a point where they have a pressing need, they cry to the parent. When they cry, they trust the parent to meet whatever the need is that they were crying about.

Furthermore, just like a parent knows the cry of their child and even the meaning of each cry, God knows the cries of His children. When they call Him, He knows exactly what they need. With the inflection of the voice, this call is very distinctively different from others. It is also typically louder than the other calls that emotional cries previously mentioned.

Call Him for Access and Power...

The final reason that I'd like to raise for one to call the name of another is that they'd like to use that name for special access or empowerment. It is an accurate idea that sometimes it's not just "what" one knows, but instead, it's about "who" one knows. Whom one knows can often give them access that would otherwise be unavailable to them. Many times it's because of the connection that the individual has with another that brings them any attention from the person they seek. Whether through a positive relationship or fear of the name one calls, the third party understands that person and gives you a favorable result.

There are some persons and pardons that one will never have access to without calling the name of Jesus. Without Jesus, we have no access to the other parts of the trinity. This is shown in Paul's letter that states, "For through him we both have access by one Spirit unto the Father." (Ephesians 2:18 KJV)

Something else that we wouldn't have access to without the name of Jesus is salvation. Luke said, "Neither is there salvation in any other: for there is none other name under heaven given among men, whereby we must be saved." (Acts 4:12 KJV) He is the only name that can save us. After committing no sin, He was wrongfully accused, detained, and beaten for crimes He did not commit. Then He went further to endure the crown, the cross, and the death just so that we could have this access. This allows His name to serve as the credential necessary for man to be saved. Paul stated in Romans that "that if thou shalt confess with thy mouth the Lord Jesus, and shalt believe in thine heart that God hath raised him from the dead, thou shalt be saved." (Romans 10:9 KJV) Because of us calling His name, we have access to this pardon.

Calling Jesus also gives us access to power. "that at the name of Jesus every knee should bow, of things in heaven, and things in earth, and things under the earth; and that every tongue should confess that Jesus Christ is Lord, to the glory of God the Father." (Philippians 2:10-11 KJV) This power is not to be used against one another. But it serves as a powerful weapon of warfare against the enemy. As believers who are authorized to use His name, we can use it cast out devils. The enemy is no match against the power of His name and has to obey when He speaks. Please note the passage that follows.

"When he saw Jesus a long way off, he ran and bowed in worship before him—then bellowed in protest, "What business do you have, Jesus, Son of the High God, messing with me? I swear to God, don't give me a hard time!" (Jesus had just commanded the tormenting evil spirit, "Out! Get out of the man!") Jesus asked him, "Tell me your name." He replied, "My name is Mob. I'm a rioting mob." Then he desperately begged Jesus not to banish them from the country." Mark 5:6-10 MSG

Here as Jesus encounters a man who has been inundated with evil spirits. They cause the man of whom they've possessed to run to Him and begged Him not to cause them to have to leave the country. They had to beg because they were aware of the power that He possesses. And as believers, we legitimately use that name to do the same great exploits that our Lord Jesus did.

Conclusion...

If we are going to be like Christ, we have to reflect Him even in our prayer lives. He often prayed to the Father and would often call unto Him while praying. "Father, forgive them," (Luke 23:34) "Oh Righteous Father," (John 17:25) "Father, let this cup pass from me." (Matthew 26:39) "Our Father, which art in heaven." (Matthew 6:9) With the privilege of relationship, our Lord and Savior, Jesus and Savior, would often call on the Father who was always there for Him. In fact, while reading the prayer of our Lord and Savior that John transcribed in chapter 17 of his Gospel, Jesus called on the Father several times during that one prayer to signify the depth of this relationship with Him.

We have to remember that we have that same privilege as we're going through. And because Christ is the mediator that exists between God and men (1 Timothy 2:5 KJV), we should never cease to call on Him. Whether through feeling, conversation, need, or access, we should never forget to call Jesus. He is the one that we rely upon. He is our very present help in times of trouble. He is our salvation. He is our healer, our deliverer, and our way maker. He is our panacea. He is our everything. He is the one. It doesn't make sense to call on someone else with this knowledge. Whether we are in trouble, feel lonely, desperate, or discouraged, we should never forget to "Call Jesus."

Prayer

Father, in the name of Jesus, we thank You for the privilege of relationship to call on You at any time. Father, we furthermore praise You because of how You've availed Yourself to us to incline Your ears unto our call. David expressed our sentiments best when he asked, "what is man that thou art mindful of him?" Even though we don't have the answer to this question, we simply want to tell You "thank You." Now, Father, we pray that You give us never to forget to call on You first. We don't want only to reflect Your image at certain times. We want to be a reliable reflection that yields that same beautiful and dependable picture of You...every time! This includes our prayer life. Lord Jesus, Give us to call Your name, just as you consistently called upon the Father. Get the glory out of our life. And Father, we love You. We thank You and Magnify You in Jesus' name. Amen

Reflection

CHAPTER SEVEN

Song of Peace

Song of Peace
Words & Music: Derrick Moore
For Soul Reaching Productions

Verse

Though the world is torn apart

There's a calm inside my heart.

It's not based on what I see

Or what's going on around me

It's from God. It's from God

Chorus

Your peace surrounds me.

Your peace encamps all around.

I'm so glad I've found peace.

Bridge

Peace that goes beyond our understanding.

Peace that guards my heart and my mind

Peace in the midst of the storm.

Shielding and protecting me from harm.

Repeat Chorus

<u>Vamp</u>

Peace. Peace. Peace. I'm thankful for your peace.

"Thou wilt keep him in perfect peace, whose mind is
stayed on thee: because he trusteth in thee."
(Isaiah 26:3 KJV)

The word peace is mentioned in the King James
Version of the bible 429 times. Though not the
most cited, it ranks as one of the most
mentioned words in scripture. One might need to take
that into consideration when determining its importance.
All who either possess it or lack it will notice its presence
and absence. This means that peace influences everyone.

Peace is a vitally important component of the
existence of all humanity. With it comes a significant level
of contentment. But on the other hand, without it, man is
most miserable. Have you ever noticed and wondered
how people with great riches could be just as troubled as
poor people? Have you ever wondered how a person with
plenty of friends can yet feel friendless? Or even wonder
how a person with a food surplus can still be hungry and
even die of starvation? Have you ever encountered a
person who is overly paranoid? These are all situations
that illustrate the absence of peace.

To better understand what peace is, one can think of it as a highway that a car rides upon. It's like a smoothly paved highway when peace is present and fully operational. The vehicle can move on it at a swift pace to arrive at a destination on time. The ride might even be so smooth until the car feels like it's gliding. In another scenario, you may have an individual walking in a partial peace that is situational. They are perfectly fine until they come face to face with a specific situation that seems to confiscate their peace. This is like riding on a smooth road, and the car suddenly comes upon a pothole in the street. When it comes to the potholes, sometimes you see them coming, and other times you don't. Depending on how deep and wide the hole is, it can damage the vehicle's tires and delay one from arriving at their destination on time. This highway is unpredictable. The driver doesn't really know what to expect when riding on it. The final scenario is one where the individual has no peace at all. This person is completely damaged and will more than likely be pessimistic about everything, including life. The best way to represent this scenario is to think of it as an unkept highway. One that is unpaved, weathered with potholes everywhere, trashed, and very rigid. This is the type of highway that is not only unpredictable. It has become a complete hazard to drive on. It can badly damage the vehicle and could even cost one their life.

Now we must understand that everyone is not the same. Neither is everyone operating at the same level of peace. There is a full spectrum by which everyone's level of peace is measured. But these three situations serve as checkpoints so that one may know and further measure where they land in the spectrum of peace.

When we assess the condition of the world in which we live, it is evident that there is a deficiency of peace. There is turmoil and danger everywhere. One can look around on any given day and see a world plagued by violence, pandemics, political division, hatred, and inflation. While these are all uncontrollable circumstances for the typical individual, they don't serve as the real problem. The problem is when what is going on externally comes inside and causes one to have internal issues.

It is prevalent that the world has internalized these troubles and succumbed to this turmoil forfeiting its peace. This is evident in the suicide rate. NAMI (National Alliance on Mental Illness) stated that the suicide rate in America has increased by 35% since 1999. They state that suicide is the 10th leading cause of death in the US. It further says that 90% of those who die by suicide have symptoms of a mental health condition. (Mental health by the numbers 2022) Even though this doesn't directly point out all the mental illnesses that plague our society, it does acknowledge that suicide is a direct result of mental illness. This stands as a strong indicator of how troubled people's minds really are.

As believers, one must remember that they are in this world but not of this world. The believer operates on a completely different system from that of the world. Because the believer relies on God and His word, they don't become so easily deterred by the storms of this life. They don't depend on this world to give them joy. If they genuinely operate according to scripture, they will not be able to omit the writings of John. He admonished the saints to "Love not the world, neither the things that are in the world. If any man love the world, the love of the Father is not in him." (1 John 2:15 KJV) At face value, many will view this as a punishment and torture to be told not to love that which they are surrounded by for however many years they are alive. But if one continues to read, they will find out that it's actually for their protection. John further wrote, "And the world passeth away, and the lust thereof: but he that doeth the will of God abideth for ever." (1 John 2:17 KJV) Here, he lets us know that God meant for His people to thrive and have longevity and not just be engulfed in pleasures that only last for a little while.

God is always consistent and never changing, while the world is inconsistent, unpredictable, and disappointing. My pastor, Dr. Gilbert Gillum, always teaches us that having the Holy Ghost allows the believer to walk in a different strength from the rest of the world. He often teaches that the Holy Ghost is "an inside brace for outside pressure." That brace pushes up against the walls of the heart and keeps it from caving in when pressure pushes against it. It allows one to continue to walk in peace.

Peace is not defined by what's going on around but rather by what's going on within. An example of this was when Jesus and His disciples were on the ship.

"And there arose a great storm of wind, and the waves beat into the ship, so that it was now full. And he was in the hinder part of the ship, asleep on a pillow: and they awake him, and say unto him, Master, carest thou not that we perish? And he arose, and rebuked the wind, and said unto the sea, Peace, be still. And the wind ceased, and there was a great calm." (Mark 4:37-39 KJV)

In the middle of the storm, Jesus was asleep. Mark says that a great storm of wind came. It was so strong that it caused the water from the sea to come onto the ship and overtake it. Though scary to the disciples, this storm didn't faze Jesus at all. He was sleeping amid the storm. Though it dominated the territory around him, it didn't disturb Him internally. This is because He had peace. Knowing who He is, we can take it a step further to say that He not only had peace, but we know that He is peace.

Peace is a tranquil state of mind that can exist during trouble. This is what allowed Jesus to have a sense of safety while danger was all around. Paul wrote in his letter to the church at Philippi and said, "And the peace of God, which passeth all understanding, shall keep your hearts and minds through Christ Jesus." (Philippians 4:7 KJV) This is what peace does. It guards and keeps the hearts and minds. It stands on guard to keep the trouble from coming in to contaminate them.

If we are to be the reflection of Christ, we must be able to face our storms just as he did. We have to be able to rest in the middle of them. It's not that the storm gives us rest. It's more so because He that is on the inside gives us peace in the midst of it. The word peace is interchangeable with the word safety. The irony is that this is saying that peace provides safety while the storm is yet raging. Another word that is interchangeable with peace is the word ease. This is saying that with peace, we have comfort while dealing with hardship. Peace makes all the difference.

If one becomes disgruntled every time they go through a storm or another unfavorable situation, they have proven to be less like Christ and more like the world. When the storm comes, it serves as the test that shows where one's mind is. That is proven in the scripture mentioned at the beginning of this chapter which states, "Thou wilt keep him in perfect peace, whose mind is stayed on thee: because he trusteth in thee." (Isaiah 26:3 KJV) When one's mind is on God, He promises to keep them in perfect peace. Therefore, if one has no peace, it is proof that their mind is not on God.

God desires that the believer be kept in perfect peace. This, according to the scripture, is a result of keeping our mind stayed on Him. He doesn't want peace to be absent or situational in the lives of those that follow Him. In a quest to be that "reliable reflection" that the world can look upon and see Christ at any time, we can't afford to be mentally or spiritually bipolar. We must pursue a consistency in God and grow in Him. This requires developing a discipline that allows one to keep their minds stayed on Him.

This is ultimately a trust thing. In fact, the scripture closes by saying, "...because he trusteth in thee." When one trusts in God, they learn to depend on Him for everything and focus on Him at all times. Peace comes automatically from the trust in this relationship. It's not something that is forced but instead forged. As one learns to trust God and draw closer to Him, they will walk in more peace.

When you walk with God, He will inundate you with peace that will prevail while you are being submerged into trouble. This is why it is one of the fruits of the spirit that are mentioned in Galatians 5:22. When God is in you, peace is inevitably produced. The song says, "Though the world is torn apart, there's a calm inside my heart." When peace is present, you don't have to tell yourself to be calm. Calm simply happens.

True peace is hard to quantify. This is because it really does go beyond our understanding. Though peace can be hard to explain thoroughly, one can recognize its presence or absence. Without it, even the simplest of things seem overbearing. But with it, the hardest of things seem simple. In the day in time that we live in, while the world is going crazy, it is more important than ever for the saints to have the peace of God.

Prayer

"Father, in the name of Jesus, we thank you for this benefit that You have made available to all that trust in You. As we look around, we see that so many need what You've made available to us. They lack Your peace. The lack of peace hasn't been this prevalent in our lifetimes. Seemingly everywhere we look, we see men troubled in their minds. Mental illness is on a rampage. It is evident more than ever that we need You. Touch the minds of Your people and give us to turn away from our distractions, for this is the only way that You can heal us and give us Your peace. More than riches, we need Your peace. More than possessions and favorable situations, we need Your peace. Forgive us for not keeping our minds on You. Forgive us for taking Your peace for granted. Forgive us and try us again. And we'll be careful to walk in that which You've given us. And we thank You for that peace in Jesus' name. Amen"

Reflection

CHAPTER EIGHT

Holding On

Holding On

Words and Music by: Derrick Moore
For Soul Reaching Publishing

Verse 1:

Though times may seem so dark and drear.

I won't fear cause I know you're near.

Your power; It never fades. Your Word; It still

remains.

So I'll keep holding on...To your unchanging hand.

Verse 2:

Burdens seem too hard for me to bear.

But You promised, You would be there cause you

care.

Your power; It never fades. Your Word; It still

remains.

So I'll keep holding on...To your unchanging hand.

Bridge:

I'm in the fight of my life, But I won't give up this

time.

I won't listen to the lies. In your word I'll abide.

You're a God of Your word...And You'll do just what

you said

I won't give up until I see everything my God

promised me.

Vamp:

Altos: I'll keep holding, I'll keep holding on.

Soprano: I'll keep holding, I'll keep holding on.

(harmonizing with alto)

Tenor: Holding on and I won't let go (3x) Holding

on. Holding on.

"And let us not be weary in well doing: for in due season we shall reap, if we faint not." (Galatians 6:9 KJV)

This very scripture is the summation of what it means to be "holding on." This phrase is often tossed around like a feather, while many cannot understand the weight that it indeed carries fully. Though simple in sound, this concept is more complex than many comprehend. If the complexity of the phrase "holding on" were apprehended by more people, perhaps less would be so quick to give up and throw in the towel. There must be three (3) major components at play for one to hold on. These components are a resolve (of dogged tenacity), a reward (or desired result), and an obstacle(s). Without either of these components being present, one can never paint a picture of what it means to be holding on.

The first of the three components is a resolve (of dogged tenacity). While growing up in the Pentecostal church, specifically the Church of God in Christ Inc., we would have a part of worship called testimony service. During this time, the saints would have the opportunity to get up individually and tell what God had done for them with the purpose of someone else hearing it and being strengthened as they go through their own trials. At the end of these testimonies, I would often hear phrases about having a mind to go on with the Lord, having a "double-determined" mind, and having no desire to turn around.

While thinking upon these testimonies, I became amazed at what the Lord revealed about them. First of all, these phrases that were spoken all speak of mindsets. This indicated that the mind serves as the seat of one's determination. It is the place where one's resolve of dogged tenacity resides. Therefore, if a person doesn't have a mind to hold on, "holding on" will never happen. Secondly, with these phrases being spoken at the end of the testimonies, we can further deduce that this mindset allowed them to be an overcomer. It also reveals that the testifier knows in their subconscious that if they want to continue being an overcomer, it is essential to maintain this same resolve for everything they were to face.

The Message version of Romans 4:18 declares that "When everything was hopeless, Abraham believed anyway," This is what the believer has to choose to do to keep holding on. One has to have this resolve in their mind when adversity is staring them in the face and even when their situation looks completely hopeless. Paul admonishes us in (1 Corinthians 15:58 KJV) to "Therefore, my beloved brethren, be ye stedfast, unmoveable, always abounding in the work of the Lord, forasmuch as ye know that your labour is not in vain in the Lord." The beginning of this verse uses the words steadfast and unmovable, which emphatically lets us know that we are to be unbending, unwavering, planted, firm, and solid. These words are all synonymous with having dogged tenacity. With this first component of holding on, having a resolution of dogged tenacity deals with having a mindset of a vicious, persistent, firm grip of hope in Christ Jesus.

The end of the previously mentioned verse mentions being steadfast and gives the reason why one is to be. It says, "...forasmuch as ye know that your labour is not in vain in the Lord." This brings us to our second component: a reward (or the desired result). This reward component of holding on makes it worth one's while. It deals with the fact that one knows that they will receive a desired result or reward if they do it. This end motivates and inspires one to keep fighting and persevering. For David even said, "I had fainted, Unless I had believed to see the goodness of the LORD in the land of the living." (Psalm 27:13 KJV) With this saying, David is acknowledging that without the hope of a reward (seeing the goodness of the Lord in the land of the living..), he would have thrown in the towel. The beautiful thing that I've learned to an extent, and am forever learning, about God is that He is a great promise keeper, fulfiller, and rewarder. There are scriptures throughout the bible that prove this infallible truth. Joshua 21:45 says, "Not one of the good promises which the Lord had spoken to the house of Israel failed; all had come to pass." (AMP)

Another example is 2 Corinthians 1:20 (KJV), which states... "For all the promises of God in him are yea, and in him Amen, unto the glory of God by us." The word also declares in Hebrews 11:6 that God "...is a rewarder of them that diligently seek Him." This second component serves as the motive by which one is holding on.

The third and final component of holding on is an obstacle. One can look forward to a desirable end and reward easily without a resolve of dogged tenacity, except there was something that complicated the situation. This complication is known as the obstacle. The obstacle can be one of many things. It can be time. Proverbs 13:12 KJV says that "Hope deferred maketh the heart sick." Time is so great of an obstacle that it has the power to make the heart sick. The obstacle can even be an internal battle. 1 Peter 4:1a (KJV) says, "Forasmuch then as Christ hath suffered for us in the flesh, arm yourselves likewise with the same mind." This acknowledges that one obstacle that will have to be dealt with is internal struggles. Another obstacle is the adversary. 1 Peter 5:8 (KJV) says to "Be sober, be vigilant; because your adversary the devil, as a roaring lion, walketh about, seeking whom he may devour." Our adversary, the devil should never be underestimated and should always be seen for the obstacle that he is. Though many more obstacles complicate the purpose and plot of one's life, these three serve as significant obstacles that all believers must face.

These three (3) components all work in harmony to make up the configuration of what "holding on" is all about. The resolve of dogged tenacity serves as the fuel. This fuel, just like a vehicle's fuel, allows one to keep going. The reward serves as the reason for holding on. Without it, holding on would seem both pointless and worthless. The final component is the obstacle. Though dreaded and intensely disliked, it serves as the vital complicating stumbling block that produces the struggle of holding on.

It's these components that are prevalent throughout the lyrics of this song. It begins by saying, "Though times may seem so dark and drear." This is the obstacle. "I won't fear cause I know You're near." This is the resolve of dogged tenacity. "Your power; it never fades. Your Word; It still remains." This is the reward. Even though the reward is not expressly stated here, those who read the Word of God realize that it is full of promises and rewards to hold on to. Then it ends with the chorus that strengthens the resolve by declaring that "I'll keep holding on."

The real question is... What do you do when your times seem dark and drear? What do you do when your burdens seem too hard to bear? Do you give up and throw in the towel? Or do you look around searching for some symbol of hope that would give you a reason to continue? If you find a symbol of hope, do you ever ask yourself if what you're holding on for is even worth the trouble?

Sometimes, doing life can seem much different from viewing principles written on paper. The reality is sometimes quitting looks easy, holding on seems impossible, and the reward doesn't seem worth it. In these times, we must pray and become one with the Word of

God. In prayer, the Lord can touch us and strengthen our resolve. It is by the revelation of God's word that we're able to understand and see how God sees. One must remain conscious that when we accept Christ into our lives, they begin a process of transformation. They start to morph through the precious blood of Jesus Christ from whoever they were into who they are meant to be. This blood changes everything about them that isn't useful to God. This includes wrong attitudes, dispositions, habits, etc. This is why we have to have an intimate relationship with God through prayer and reading the word. The two of these together allow one to be transformed into the reflection of Christ.

Prayer

"Father, I pray that You help us. Help us to understand that Your will is what's best for us. Though it may not always be easy to walk in it, it's still worth holding on to. Some are holding on trying to make it through a tough season in their lives. Some are trying to find the strength to hold on through the loss of a loved one. Some are trying to hold on until they receive that financial blessing or miraculous healing. At the same time, others are simply searching for the strength to hold on to You. Help us, Lord! You said in Your word that if we faint in the day of adversity, our strength is small. So, Lord, we pray today that You increase our strength. Help us go through this uncomfortable place in this journey of becoming more like You. We want to look like You, love like You, and be like You. We thank you for strengthening our resolve, not letting us forget about the reward, and helping us overcome every obstacle that we face. In Jesus' name. Amen."

Reflection

CHAPTER NINE

Well Done

Well Done

Words & Music: Derrick Moore
For Soul Reaching Productions

Verse

Baritone: Coming so soon. Coming so soon.

Tenors: Coming so soon. Coming so soon.

Altos & Sopranos: He's coming again so soon.

Maybe morning night or noon. He's coming! He's

coming!

Chorus

Be ready when the trumpet sounds.

Don't wait but do it now.

I don't want to hear Him say depart.

But I want to hear Him say well done.

Repeat Verse

Repeat Chorus

Organ Interlude

Vamp

Well Done! Good and Faithful Servant

Well Done!

Ending

Enter in the Joy of the Lord

"His Lord said unto him, Well done, thou good and faithful servant: thou hast been faithful over a few things, I will make thee ruler over many things: enter thou into the joy of thy Lord." (Matthew 25:21 KJV)

There are two words that all who have heard of Heaven generally want to hear when they stand before the judgement bar of God. These words are "Well Done." They know that these will be the words that the Lord utters for all who will be able to access eternal life and live in heaven with Him forever. The alternative of hearing this will be hearing Him say, "...I never knew you: depart from me, ye that work iniquity." (Matthew 7:23b KJV) According to Matthew 25:30, the one that hears these words will be cast into outer darkness where there will be weeping and gnashing of teeth. This is the unfavorable judgment.

Everyone in their right mind wants to hear the Lord say, "Well Done." The complication lies in the fact that many expect it to be automatic. Many are walking in false expectations concerning heaven. Since the onset of the COVID-19 pandemic, most of the world has been touched by the death of a loved one at the hand of the virus. I've seen individuals die who never confessed Christ as Lord and savior and even some who didn't believe in His existence. What caused me to be disgruntled was seeing others post their passing on social media. They would often end their posts by saying, "RIH" (Rest in Him), "I know that you're enjoying heaven," "God has another angel in heaven with Him," and many other similar sayings. What bothered me most was that many of these sayings came from believers who often knew the individual's life. This caused me to question why they would say things like that. Did they run out of things to say and simply decided to say what seemed to fit? Or even more dangerously, do they not know what the Bible says about heaven and those who will be able to inherit it?

So many call heaven their eternal home but aren't making any preparations to go there. They don't take into consideration that heaven is indeed a prepared place for a prepared people. Peter wrote, "And if it is difficult for the righteous to be saved, what will become of the godless and the sinner?" (1 Peter 4:18 AMP) This lets me know that the unrighteous don't stand a chance. If the believer intends to make it in, they must walk in total obedience to the truth of Christ. If one intends to serve the God of the

Bible and reap the results written in it, they must follow its instructions.

The Bible gives specific instructions concerning those who desire to go to heaven. Revelations 20:11-15 lets us know that all of humankind will have to stand before the great white throne of God and be judged according to their works written in the books. These books will hold the records of the works that man has done.

Along with the other books that will be present, there will be the book of life. Those whose names were not found in the book of life were cast into the lake of fire along with death and hell. The names written in the book of life are only those who received God's gift to man-His son Jesus. "For God so loved the world, that he gave his only begotten Son, that whosoever believeth in him should not perish, but have everlasting life." (John 3:16 KJV) He came so that we could be saved and have everlasting life. This is only obtainable by accepting Him as Lord and Savior according to the scripture that says, "that if thou shalt confess with thy mouth the Lord Jesus, and shalt believe in thine heart that God hath raised him from the dead, thou shalt be saved. For with the heart man believeth unto righteousness; and with the mouth confession is made unto salvation." (Romans 10:9-10 KJV) Though many try to bypass the word's instructions and do their own thing, in the end, the Word of God will be the only thing that stands.

Since the early 2000s, a fad has been going around of people uttering the words "Only God can judge me." They even became so bold that they often had it tattooed on their bodies. This urban campaign began as a response to unwelcome criticism of one's actions, attitude, clothing, or disposition. The problem is that most who take this mindset upon themselves aren't prepared for God's judgment. They simply declare this because the judgement of the Lord is delayed and not currently before them. The Bible speaks of this when it says, "Because sentence against an evil work is not executed speedily, therefore the heart of the sons of men is fully set in them to do evil." (Ecclesiastes 8:11 KJV) This is one instance where delayed doesn't mean denied. Just because judgment hasn't come yet doesn't mean that it isn't coming.

No number of social media likes or approvals given by any man can override the word of God. The reality is everything that exists only exists because God allows it to. God gave man the knowledge of creating and operating the social media sites. Man's every breath is in the hands of God. Without Him, man is nothing. Therefore, it makes no sense to seek to please a man when we should be seeking to please and obey God.

His word not only tells us how to get our names written in the book of life. It also tells us how the other books will judge us. He lets us know that it will be by our works. This is one concept that man doesn't often take under consideration. When Jesus was telling the parable in Matthew 25 and mentioned that the Lord would say "Well done," this was only because the servant actually "did well." They that intend to go to heaven have to work. In fact, Jesus often accompanied parables concerning one making it into the kingdom of heaven with serving and doing work.

One parable that He told was that spoken of at the beginning of this chapter extracted from Matthew 25. This parable speaks of a lord who gives his servants his goods according to their abilities with the expectation to make a profit. Those who did it heard the lord say to them, "Well done," and received a reward. The one who didn't profit was the one that the lord called wicked and slothful and received punishment.

Another parable He told was of an estate owner in Matthew 20 who found laborers at different times of the day. They all agreed to work for a penny a day regardless of what hour they started. This showed that no matter how early or late it is in one's life, it's not too late to start and receive the reward of Heaven.

Our Lord and Savior was trying to let us know that we have an obligation to work. If there is no work, there is no reason to say, "Well done." This makes perfect sense considering "well done" is just another way of saying "good job." Therefore, one should work all they can while they have a chance. Whether it seems like it or not, my Bible lets me know that every man shall be judged according to his works.

If people remained aware that they will be judged according to their works, maybe they would approach the work differently. Instead of being caught up in this worldly system that seems to be dominating right now, they would be making sure to do whatever their hands could find to do for the upbuilding of the kingdom. (Ecclesiastes 9:10 KJV) I'm also convinced that people would complain less about doing the Lord's work and invest more effort into making sure they are serving the Lord with gladness.

It is evident that many don't realize that they are getting paid for their work for God. That's why specific phrases, though sensible in secularism, shouldn't be used among the believer. One of these words is volunteerism. Many take on the mindset of a volunteer and use it as a banner by which they can give God half-hearted service as they see fit. This concept is not biblical. We, as believers, are laborers. We are not volunteers. As a laborer in the Gospel, God demands that we work in the spirit of excellence with Him in mind. Paul wrote of this in one of his letters and said, "And whatsoever ye do, do it heartily, as to the Lord, and not unto men;" (Colossians 3:23 KJV)

Interestingly, Paul didn't stop there. He went further to write, "But he that doeth wrong shall receive for the wrong which he hath done: and there is no respect of persons." (Colossians 3:25 KJV) He was letting them know that God is going to judge every man. They who do good shall receive a reward, while they who do wrong shall receive punishment for their works. He closes by making known that God has no respect of persons. No man is exempt from the judgement of God.

With the amount of noise in the earth that tells you that everything is acceptable as long as people accept you, we must be careful not to listen to it. We, as believers, must abide in the unwavering truth of God. His word is the truth. (John 17:17) His word tells us that we must receive Him as our Lord and savior and work the works of Him that sent us to make it in. There are no exceptions to the word of God.

It is for this cause that we seek diligently to please Him. This is why we remain "joyful in hope, patient in affliction, and faithful in prayer." (Romans 12:12 NIV) This is why we serve the Lord untiringly and with all our hearts. This is why we press through our troubles, trials, temptations, and tribulations. This is why we love those who mistreat us. This is why we continue to fast and pray. This is why we are pushing to go all the way. We are laborers that are working to receive our reward. Heaven is our goal.

I'll never forget the words of the late Bishop GE Patterson, who spoke of his thoughts by acknowledging that he wasn't abstaining from specific actions simply because he loved God. He said he was afraid to do certain things because he was "hell-scared." I agree with Bishop

Patterson. Though my love for God is continuing to grow, I don't have to be corrected about certain things because I, too, am "hell-scared." I do it all because I want to have the testimony of Paul when he said, "I have fought a good fight, I have finished my course, I have kept the faith: henceforth there is laid up for me a crown of righteousness, which the Lord, the righteous judge, shall give me at that day: and not to me only, but unto all them also that love his appearing." (2 Timothy 4:7-8 KJV) I want to go to heaven when I die. And the only way I can gain that access is if He sees my name written in the book of life when I stand before that great white throne. Then He will utter the words that I've longed to hear all my life. "Well Done."

Prayer

"Father, in the name of Jesus, we come to You repenting for our slothfulness and bad disposition concerning Your work. We thank You for Your revelation that brings us back into proper alignment with You. Thank You for thinking enough of us to show us the error of our ways and give us the strength to correct our wrongdoings. We commit to working the works of Him that sent us while it is day. We know that night is coming and that all work will then cease. We want to please You, Lord. And because we want our names written in that book of life, we pray that You forgive us of our sins. Blot out our transgressions. We receive You as our Lord and Savior. Now, Lord, we pray that You take pleasure in the work and worship that resonates from our hands and hearts. We pray that You receive it, and at the end of the day declare, "Well Done, thou good and faithful servant." In Jesus' Name. Amen"

Reflection

CHAPTER TEN

Conclusion

I remember praying to the Lord concerning something that I felt was very urgent. I prayed in a panicking manner from my place of desperation. I was anxiously dealing with a need that seemed to plague me at that moment. It left me crying with my heart beating nervously fast as I prayed to the Lord about it. It appeared to be so great.

When the Lord responded to me, He first repeated only one word. He began to say "Peace! Peace! Peace!" After hearing the Lord utter these words audibly, He then spoke to my spirit. He told me to calm down and know that He (the Lord) is able. He continued to let me know in a gentle way that I was becoming pressed for nothing—informing me that my issue was pressing because I treated it as if it had to be solved before He left me by myself. Finally, the Lord reminded me that this is not a one-night stand but that we were here together for the long haul. We are married.

Through these words, He let me know that there is no reason to be anxious in my prayers. Scripture even confirms this when it's *"Be careful (anxious) for nothing; but in every thing by prayer and supplication with thanksgiving let your requests be made known unto God."*

(Philippians 4:6 KJV) While praying, I couldn't even get into the thanksgiving part because I was anxious. I was praying frantically. After the Lord spoke to me and calmed me, He was able to deal appropriately with my need.

Though I received an answered prayer from that exchange, I believe that the lessons I learned gave me so much more. In hindsight, I can see how when one becomes anxious while praying, as did I, it's generally because the individual questions God's ability, willingness, or timing. This shows a lack of trust. Either we don't trust Him to do it, or we don't trust Him to do it by the time that it's necessary to be done. This anxiety even shows that we question His love, omniscience, and omnipotence.

It shows that we question His love in the same manner that the disciples questioned it when Jesus slept in the hinder part of the ship while the storm was raging. They even went to Him and asked, "Do you not care that we are about to die?" (Mark 4:38 AMP) This is the epitome of an anxiety prayer. After they woke Jesus up, He said, "Peace be still!" and rebuked the wind and the sea. This was when He looked at His disciples and said, "...Why are ye so fearful? how is it that ye have no faith?"

(Mark 4:40b KJV) Their prayer in this manner caused Jesus to call them faithless.

Through both my situation and that of the disciples, we questioned the Lord's dependability. Neither case said we weren't believers, but both scenarios showed that we had a moment of unbelief.

His dependability is what allows us to take our burdens to Him and leave them at His feet. He is more than capable of handling any and every situation that we bring to him. We can trust Him to fulfill every word He has spoken to us. He declares in His word that *"God is not a man, that he should lie; Neither the son of man, that he should repent: Hath he said, and shall he not do it? Or hath he spoken, and shall he not make it good?"* (Numbers 23:19 KJV) There has never been a valid question concerning God's dependability. The word is inundated with examples of his perfect record of delivering and coming through for His people.

God's dependability can be characterized by Him being unfailing, faithful, trustworthy, and reliable. These characteristics specify that whatever God is, that's what He forever shall be. No matter how amazing He is today,

He will be just as fantastic tomorrow. No matter how He demonstrated His grace, power, or love today, He will display the same characteristics tomorrow. He will forever be God. *"Jesus Christ the same yesterday, and to day, and for ever."* (Hebrew 13:8) God is reliable! He is truly excellent!

As a minister of music and church administrator, I teach that excellence has little to do with the ability to plan something and do it right once. Excellence has more to do with the ability to do it right so many times that it's virtually impossible to do it wrong. This is why I boldly declare that God is excellent. He doesn't make mistakes. He doesn't get it wrong—ever.

As a reflection of Christ, I have that same obligation. I must be excellent. Many settle for working hard and planning to do it right once. They settle for looking like Christ only on certain days of the week or in front of specific individuals. These individuals work hard to appear excellent, but this is nothing more than a performance in reality. It is not excellence.

What God is desirous of is someone willing to be a reliable reflection. Have you ever looked in a specific type of mirror and hated how it portrayed your image? Some mirrors enhance your image, while others can even distort it. You might want to stand in front of the mirror that enhances your image if you need a confidence booster. The mirror that distorts your image will likely only be used to give you a good laugh. These mirrors are curved. This curviness of its makeup allows the light to bend uniquely to provide an enhanced image of whatever is in front of it. This is not what the Lord desires when He wants to see Himself.

When God looks for His reflection, He looks for what can be seen in a plane mirror. A plane mirror lets light reflect off of it evenly. This is what gives you an object's "true" reflection. God doesn't need enhancements. He simply needs a reliable reflection. He is looking for someone who will always allow light to reflect on them evenly so that He is always seen.

He doesn't want someone that can look like Him on Sundays but look like someone else on Monday. He is desirous of someone that shows forth His reflection at any given moment. He is seeking excellence.

For what good is a reflection if it's not reliable. Think about a doctor who uses an unreliable blood pressure machine to measure a patient's blood pressure. If the doctor accepted the readings of the faulty device and prescribed the patient medicine based on the readings of that defective blood pressure machine, it would cause an adverse outcome for the patient. The doctor could prescribe the wrong medication or give the wrong dosage to that patient. Rather than helping the patient, this can hurt them, make them sicker, or even kill them.

This metaphor is exact in that it shows our need to be a reliable reflection. If we prove to be an unreliable reflection of Christ, someone can look upon us and take an inaccurate measurement. They can falsely measure some of our actions, thinking that they are the ways of Christ. If that individual looks upon us and considers our actions acceptable, they can pattern their lives after the raggedy lives they see us living. This can cause that individual harm and even destruction in the end.

When we become Christ's reflection, we must remain cognizant that we are not doing it because He needs flattery. God is God. He was God before man ever existed and would continue being God even if man were gone. He wants us to be His reflection so that others can see Him and be converted to believe in who He is. So when we fail to be a reliable reflection, we are not hindering God. We are hindering someone else from seeing God. If that individual doesn't see God, they may never be able to escape from the grips of whatever is going on in their lives. They will never be able to walk in the wholeness that God has ordained for them.

Many people don't consider the end of unreliable objects when they tend to be unreliable. Think about the things you possess or even the people in your life that prove unreliable. What do you usually do with those things or people? The reality is that anything or anyone that proves unreliable eventually won't be trusted, won't be used, and will soon be discarded. This is the reason that Jesus cursed the fig tree in Mark 11. The tree was unreliable to produce figs for those who needed it. God requires us to be just as He was.

He is looking for us to be excellent and reliable in the way that we portray Him for others to see. Are you a one-hit-wonder when it comes to reflecting Christ, or are you striving for the excellence that is required? Are you providing a clear reflection of who Christ is? Is the reflection distorted by the habits that you refuse to give up? Are you a reliable reflection, or is it all just a performance for a particular day or a specific audience?

Now that we've established what a reflection is and what it means to be a reliable reflection for Christ, you must make up your mind to be it. You have to make up your to either begin or push through this transitional period. This book was not designed to honor you for the years of saying that you've been in the faith. It's written to challenge you to be an excellent and valuable instrument God can use in the earth. A vessel that God can look at and see an undistorted image of himself at any given time. It doesn't matter how long you've been saved or even claimed salvation without ever living the life that should accompany it; God yet desires you to make up your mind this day to receive what He has for you. He wants to give you a moment that will initiate your experience of transformation from who you were into whom He's called you to be from the beginning.

It doesn't matter how far you've gone from God or even how long you've been drifting from Him. You must know that He has not changed His mind about you. God still loves you. His plan to do great things on the earth yet includes you if you only surrender your all to Him. All that

He desires from you is an unwavering "Yes. A yes that supersede temptation, personal desires, and unfavorable circumstances. He wants a yes that causes you to realize that it's not about you but the glory (light) that is given to Him that would allow others to look at us and see his "REFLECTION."

Prayer

"Father, in the name of Jesus, I pray for every reader of this book. Show them, through this book, that you are great and desire to be great in their lives. Let them know that you still have great plans for them despite all of their failures. I bind the condemnation of the enemy but speak forth the conviction of Christ. The conviction that softens and penetrates hearts that have been seared. God, You're able! Help them make up their minds to serve You unwaveringly with all of their heart. Lord let them know that they weren't created just to enjoy the pleasures of this world but that You created them for Your glory and that they are to live our lives unto You. Give them to live for You every minute of the day. Give every reader to be a reflection of Your glory at all times. One that is pleasing in Your sight. We're ready! Transform us! We say, "Yes Lord!" In Jesus' name, we pray, Amen."

Reflection

Bibliography

Dictionary.com. (n.d.). Dictionary.com. Retrieved December 10, 2022, from https://www.dictionary.com/

Mental health by the numbers. NAMI. (2021, March). Retrieved November 19, 2021, from https://www.nami.org/mhstats

The Bible. Amplified Version. YouVersion, version 42, You Version / 2021.

The Bible. King James Version. YouVersion, version 42, You Version / 2021.

The Bible. Message Version. YouVersion, version 42, You Version / 2021.

The Bible. New International Version. YouVersion, version 42, You Version / 2021.

Reflection

Acknowledgments

I am a firm believer in the saying that no man is an island. It takes all of us to make one of us. I am a product of all that the Lord has blessed me to be surrounded by. With the Lord telling me to write this book. I had no clue what to do. But while writing, He revealed to me that He had already given me everything I needed.

This word was spoken to me years ago by Stephen Black. Man of God, thank you for being a true vessel that is bold enough to speak what God said even when I didn't see it.

To Consuela Jackson and Aubrette Davis, thank you for allowing me to utilize your editorial discernment. Thank you for the encouraging words and for pointing me in the right direction and to the right tools to push this through. I am so grateful.

To my Pastor and First Lady. Pastor Gilbert and Lady Louise Gillum. It was the Lord's will for me to move to Waco and I am grateful that He blessed me with two great leaders. I'm appreciative of my First Lady's warm words that are always so encouraging and the helping hand that she always offers. And what all can I say about my Pastor. He really is a man after God's own heart. For the countless times that his sermons, personal words, and prayers have encouraged and lifted. One of the greatest honors of my life was for my pastor, Dr. Gilbert Gillum Jr., to pen the forward of this book. That is something I will never forget. I am so grateful for the Godly leadership that He has afforded me the opportunity to be under.

About the Author

Elder Derrick Maurice Moore was born on December 11, 1985, in Forrest City, AR. He is the seventh of eleven children born to Fred and Mary Moore. He gave his life to the Lord at the age of 9 at his home church, Day's Temple C.O.G.I.C., under the leadership of the late-Bishop John Henry Jennings.

After receiving the Lord, Derrick learned to play the organ through dreams given by the spirit. While cultivating this gift, he served as organist and minister of music for five years at Day's Temple. Moore also served as the Jurisdictional Chief Organist of the Arkansas 1st Jurisdiction of his denomination, the Church of God in Christ, for seven years under the leadership of the late-Bishop L.T. Walker, appointed at the age of 14 years old.

Derrick attended and graduated from Forrest City High School and attended Arkansas State University for three years. He majored in vocal music education until he moved to Waco, Texas, by the leading of the Lord in 2007. In December of 2013, he graduated with an Associate degree from McLennan Community College in

Business Management. In May of 2018, he graduated with his Bachelor's degree from Tarleton State University.

After moving to Waco, TX, in May of 2007, Derrick began his tenure serving as the Minister of Music of the Living Word C.O.G.I.C. under the leadership of the visionary pastor, Dr. Gilbert Gillum Jr. Since living in Waco, he has served in many different capacities including: district minister of music of the Greater Waco District, music director for the Texas Southwest Jurisdiction for ten years, music director for Louisiana Greater New Orleans Jurisdiction, as well as the Church Administrator and Chief of Staff of the Living Word C.O.G.I.C. Eld. Moore currently serves as the Minister of Music for Texas Covenant Assembly of Churches.

Through the years, Derrick has been afforded the opportunity to play at the major national conventions for his denomination, the Church of God in Christ. He has also been able to play for and work with several artists and Gospel notables, including Yolanda Adams, Dorinda Clark-Cole, Douglas Miller, Norman Hutchins, Chrystal Rucker, Twinkie Clark, Beverly Crawford, Kathy Taylor, Judith Christie-McAllister, Professor Iris Stevenson, and many more.

In 2012, Eld. Moore was allowed to lead his local church choir, The Living Word C.O.G.I.C. Mass Choir, in their first-ever recording titled "Live in Waco" under the visionary leadership of his pastor, Dr. Gilbert Gillum Jr. On February 16, 2021, the Lord graced him and a group of "Friends" to release his first single entitled "Holding On." On February 25, 2022, by the leading of the Holy Ghost, he will release his first book and complete album. Both are entitled "Reflection."

In Waco, while in prayer, the Lord revealed to him His call to minister the word saying, "PREACH, PREACH, PREACH HOLINESS!!! Many shall be delivered, healed, and set free."

Throughout life, Elder Moore accredits his aspirations to the examples set by his parents, the legacy of the late Bishop John Henry and Mother Matlena Jennings, as well as a host of other saints that have gone before him. He desires to please the Lord with all his heart, mind, and soul.